Toni Morrison's

Beloved

Text by
Gail Rae Rosensfit
(M.A. Hunter College)
Department of English
McKee Vocational Technical High School
Staten Island, New York

Illustrations by
Karen Pica

Research & Education Association

What **MAXnotes**™ *Will Do for You*

This book is intended to help you absorb the essential contents and features of Toni Morrison's *Beloved* and to help you gain a thorough understanding of the work. The book has been designed to do this more quickly and effectively than any other study guide.

For best results, this **MAXnotes** book should be used as a companion to the actual work, not instead of it. The interaction between the two will greatly benefit you.

To help you in your studies, this book presents the most up-to-date interpretations of every section of the actual work, followed by questions and fully explained answers that will enable you to analyze the material critically. The questions also will help you to test your understanding of the work and will prepare you for discussions and exams.

Meaningful illustrations are included to further enhance your understanding and enjoyment of the literary work. The illustrations are designed to place you into the mood and spirit of the work's settings.

The **MAXnotes** also include summaries, character lists, explanations of plot, and section-by-section analyses. A biography of the author and discussion of the work's historical context will help you put this literary piece into the proper perspective of what is taking place.

The use of this study guide will save you the hours of preparation time that would ordinarily be required to arrive at a complete grasp of this work of literature. You will be well prepared for classroom discussions, homework, and exams. The guidelines that are included for writing papers and reports on various topics will prepare you for any added work which may be assigned.

The **MAXnotes** will take your grades "to the max."

Dr. Max Fogiel
Program Director

Contents

> **Each page range includes List of Characters,
> Summary, Analysis, Study Questions and
> Answers, and Suggested Essay Topics.**

Introduction

The Life and Work of Toni Morrison

Toni Morrison was born Chloe Anthony Wofford on February 18, 1931, in Lorain, Ohio. Her parents, Ramah (Willis) and George, survived the Great Depression with the aid of government assistance and by sharing with their equally poor black and white neighbors. Her great-grandmother had been a slave and her grandfather was born in slavery, not being freed until he was five, when the Emancipation Proclamation became law.

Ms. Morrison earned a B.A. in English from Howard University in 1953 and, while a student there, changed her name to Toni. She also joined the Howard Players during her undergraduate years and toured the South, playing to mostly black audiences. Her M.A. was earned in 1955 at Cornell University; her thesis was on the theme of suicide in the works of William Faulkner and Virginia Woolf. She moved to Texas Southern University, where she became an instructor of English from 1955 to 1957. There she wrote a play entitled "Dreaming Emmett" which dealt with the 1955 lynching of 14-year-old Emmett Till. Ms. Morrison returned to Howard University to be an Instructor of English for the next seven years and began writing. During that time, in 1958, she married a Jamaican architect, Harold Morrison. Two sons were born during this six-year marriage. After divorcing her husband, she took her sons back to Lorain to their grandparents' home. The next year, she became an editor for the textbook subsidiary of Random House in Syracuse, New York.

Five years later, in 1970, her first novel, *The Bluest Eye*, was published and Ms. Morrison took an editorial position at Random

House's New York office, where she eventually became a senior editor. During this time—1971 and 1972—she was also an Associate Professor of English at the State University of New York–Purchase. In 1974, *Sula*, her second novel, was published and she edited *The Black Book*, a collection of memorabilia from three hundred years of black history, which contained the Margaret Garner story—the springboard for *Beloved*. Upon the publishing of *The Black Book*, Ms. Morrison wrote an article entitled "Rediscovering Black History." The following year, *Sula* was nominated for the National Book Award. For the next two years, she was a visiting lecturer at Yale University. In 1977, her third novel, *Song of Solomon*, for which she received the National Book Critics' Circle Award and the American Academy and Institute of Arts and Letter Award, was published and quickly became a paperback best seller with 570,000 copies in print. Ms. Morrison was then named Distinguished Writer of 1978 by the American Academy of Arts and Letters. *Tar Baby*, her fourth novel, published in 1981, was on the *New York Times* best seller list for four months. During this time, Ms. Morrison was on the cover of *Newsweek*.

From 1984 to 1989, Ms. Morrison was the Schweitzer Professor of Humanities at the State University of New York–Albany and won numerous honors. In 1986, her play was produced by the Capitol Repertory Company and she won the New York State Governor's Art Award. The following year, *Beloved*—which was dedicated to the 60 million who died in slavery—was published and nominated for both the National Book Award and the National Book Critics' Award. In 1986, Ms. Morrison won the Pulitzer Prize in Fiction as well as the Robert F. Kennedy Award for this fifth novel. In 1989, Ms. Morrison became the Robert F. Goheen Professor of Humanities at Princeton University, where she teaches both creative writing and Afro-American Studies. *Jazz*, which is her sixth novel, and her non-fiction *Playing in the Dark: Whiteness and the Literary Imagination*, were published in 1992.

Toni Morrison has been featured on the Public Broadcasting System's *Writers in America*, London Weekend Television's *South Bank Show*, and Swiss Television Production's *In Black and White*. She was appointed to President Carter's National Council of the Arts and elected to the American Academy and Institute of Arts and Letters. Many books of interpretation and criticism have been written about her novels. Her own novels have been translated into German, Spanish, French, Finnish, and Italian and are taught in Afro-American, American Literature, and Women's Studies courses.

Historical Background

In July of 1862, President Lincoln announced the Emancipation Proclamation, freeing all slaves. In 1865, the Civil War between the states, basically fought over the slavery issue, had ended. By 1871, all the states were once again part of the federal government. However, some of the states were slow to accept the now-freed slaves. Although they were free, random violence against them was still commonplace: lynching, rape, beating. Concurrently, blacks were still judging each other through white values, such as monetary worth and "uppityness." At the same time, the blacks who had established their own Underground Railroad during slavery continued to help. Most blacks, along with the poor whites with whom they shared the community, worked together assisting without waiting to be asked but as a matter of course, preaching, urging on, and sharing.

The flashback portions of *Beloved* take place in Kentucky, a border state during the Civil War, and one which practiced slavery as exemplified in Sweet Home (after schoolteacher comes to take the deceased Mr. Garner's place) where Sethe was a slave 16 years before the story begins. Kentucky is also the state south of Ohio. The book's present takes place in Cincinnati, Ohio, Ms. Morrison's home state (although not her home city) eight years after the end of the Civil War.

The novel is based upon the Margaret Garner incident that Ms. Morrison read about when she edited *The Black Book*. In 1855, Mrs. Garner escaped slavery in Kentucky and fled to Cincinnati, Ohio, to live with her mother-in-law, who was a preacher. She brought her four children out of slavery with her. When she realized that a slave catcher had found them, she killed her daughter by slitting her throat, attempted to murder her two sons by beating in their heads with a shovel, and also attempted to murder her infant daughter by slamming her against a wall. All this was done in a shed behind her mother-in-law's house while the slave catcher was approaching. Her reason for the attempted murders of her children was that she would rather have them dead than alive in slavery as she had been.

Master List of Characters

Sethe—*the protagonist of the novel; a former slave.*

Beloved—*possibly the twenty-year-old reincarnation of Sethe's two-year-old daughter.*

Denver—*Sethe's living daughter.*

Baby Suggs—*Sethe's mother-in-law, who was the spiritual leader of the Cincinnati community.*

Howard and Buglar—*Sethe's two sons who ran away—first one, then the other—as soon as they reached their teens.*

Paul D—*one of the several male slaves at Sweet Home when Sethe was a slave there.*

Stamp Paid—*an older, former slave who ferried Sethe and the newborn Denver over the river to freedom.*

Lady Jones—*a light-skinned, yellow-haired black who is the school teacher in Cincinnati.*

The Bodwins—*brother and sister; rented the house at 124 Bluestone Road to Baby Suggs, and after her death to Sethe.*

Halle—*Sethe's husband.*

Mr. Garner—*owner of Sweet Home.*

Mrs. Garner—*Mr. Garner's wife.*

Sixo—*another of the male slaves at Sweet Home.*

schoolteacher—*Mr. Garner's brother-in-law; came to manage Sweet Home at Mrs. Garner's request after her husband's death.*

Sawyer—*the owner of the restaurant where Sethe works as a cook.*

Janey Wagon—*a freed black woman who works for the Bodwins.*

Ella—*a member of the Underground Railroad who responded to Stamp Paid's signal when Sethe and Denver arrived.*

Thirty-Mile Woman—*Sixo's love and the mother of his unborn child.*

Summary of the Novel

Mr. and Mrs. Garner owned Sweet Home, a farm where they used the slave labor of Paul F, Halle, Paul A, Paul D, and Sixo—although they treated their slaves with a modicum of respect, asking for their ideas and allowing them the use of rifles for hunting. Sethe, a young female slave, was bought and allowed to choose Halle for her husband. With the Garners' permission, the two slaves were "married." They had a family of two sons and a daughter before Mr. Garner became ill and died.

Prior to his death, Mr. Garner had allowed Halle the privilege of hiring his labor out so that he could buy his mother, Baby Suggs, out of slavery. At 60 years of age, Halle's mother was a free woman and moved to the next state north, Ohio, where she rented 124 Bluestone Road from the anti-slavery Bodwins and became a spiritual leader (rather than a preacher since she preferred not to preach) and a mender of shoes.

After her husband's death, the weak-willed Mrs. Garner became very ill. She complied when she was told she must have other whites in residence and invited schoolteacher and his two nephews to live with her and manage the farm, including the slaves. Schoolteacher and his nephews were a different breed than the Garners and introduced whippings, torture, humiliation, and the dehumanizing of the slaves, but Mrs. Garner was too ill to take heed. The slaves (with the exception of Paul F, who had been sold two years prior for the money needed to keep up the farm) decided to flee via the Underground Railroad. Sethe, pregnant again, had sent her two-year-old daughter and two older sons ahead with some of the other slaves when her husband, Halle, did not arrive to meet them in the predetermined place at the predetermined time.

She stayed behind to look for him but was caught by schoolteacher's nephews who held her down and sucked milk from her breasts. Schoolteacher discovered that she told Mrs. Garner about the incident and whipped her, flaying open the skin of her back despite her being six month's pregnant.

Unbeknownst to Sethe, her husband was in hiding in the loft where he had a view of the attack on her. Watching without being able to come to her aid drove him insane. Paul D was watching

Halle, although unable to see what was happening to Sethe. At some undetermined time soon after, he saw Halle sit down and calmly smear the butter from the churn all over his face while his eyes remained vacant. Sethe managed to escape, but had to stop because her baby was being born. An indentured servant, Amy, happened upon her and helped her. The infant was named Denver, which was Amy's last name.

Sethe reached her mother-in-law's home with the newborn infant and was overjoyed to be reunited with her other three children. Soon after, Baby Suggs and Sethe hosted a picnic-barbecue for all the neighbors. The abundance of food and good times, in addition to Baby Suggs' good fortune in having been bought out of slavery, driven to freedom in a wagon by her former master, and befriended by the Bodwins who rented her their two-story house (unlike the one-story houses everyone else lived in), led the neighbors and friends, who also were Baby Suggs' congregation, to believe she and her family were "uppity." Thereafter, the residents of 124 Bluestone Road found themselves being shunned until they no longer had any visitors and Baby Suggs stopped being the spiritual leader at the clearing in the woods.

Schoolteacher, one of his nephews, the sheriff, and a slave catcher arrived to bring Sethe and her children back to Sweet Home. No one had warned them but Sethe recognized schoolteacher's hat as he approached the house on his horse. She whisked her children into the shed and attempted to murder them, rather than allow them to live the kind of life in slavery she had led, as both her mother-in-law and Stamp Paid stood in the yard behind the house, frozen in terror. She succeeded in killing her two-year-old daughter by slitting her throat and would have also killed her infant daughter, Denver, if Stamp Paid had not caught the baby as Sethe swung her against the wall in an attempt to bash her brains out. The two boys had been severely beaten on their heads with a shovel.

Howard and Buglar were nursed back to health by their grandmother while Sethe was jailed to await her trial for the murder. Since Denver was still a suckling infant, she went to jail with her mother. The Bodwins used whatever influence they had in Cincinnati to ensure Sethe's imprisonment, rather than the death sentence. They were successful.

After serving her sentence, Sethe and Denver returned to Baby Suggs' home to join her, Howard, and Buglar. Once there, it was apparent that the spirit of the murdered child was haunting the house. Howard and Buglar were so affected by this that each left home as he reached his teens. Sethe found work cooking for most of the day at Sawyer's restaurant: the owner was not afraid to hire an ex-convict. However, the rest of the community, except for Stamp Paid, continued to avoid the family.

Denver, a lonely and very quiet child, was brought up in the house with her mother and grandmother. When she was seven, she discovered that Lady Jones was teaching the local children in her home and joined the classes, only to leave when one of the children innocently asked Denver about the murder of her older sister. Baby Suggs decided to die, despite Stamp Paid's efforts to dissuade her, and did after keeping close to her house or in her bed for many years. Her death came soon after Howard and Buglar left, but had nothing to do with their departure.

Eighteen years after the murder, Paul D arrives in town. He, too, had attempted to flee Sweet Home but was caught in the attempt and forced to wear an iron bit which holds down the tongue—a form of torture and humiliation. He had been sold to Brandywine, the man he soon tried to kill. The murder attempt led to his imprisonment in the worst possible type of work–gang prison in Alfred, Georgia. He escaped from the prison and stayed with the Cherokee until he was the only escaped prisoner left out of the original forty-six. The Cherokee showed him how to follow the trees to the north, which he did. Eventually he reached Delaware, where he stayed for eighteen months with a woman who had been kind to him. Once he left her, he was rootless until he came to Sethe's home.

Upon finding Sethe, he is dismayed to hear of Baby Suggs' death and—despite Denver's hostility—moves into the house. On the first night there, he has a confrontation with the spirit in the house and wins, thereby effectively sending away Denver's only companion for the last eighteen years and practically wrecking Sethe's kitchen. In an effort to win both Sethe and Denver over, he talks them into going to colored day at the carnival. When they return home, they discover a young, very tired, nattily dressed black woman waiting for them. Sethe immediately discerns that she is her daughter's spirit reborn in the flesh. Paul D and Denver see only that the girl needs sleep and water.

Beloved, who seems to have no memory other than her name, is incorporated into the household, much to Paul D's chagrin. She becomes devoted to Sethe, following her from room to room and even meeting Sethe after work once she regains her strength. Beloved's obvious interest in seducing Paul D makes him so uncomfortable he moves into the shed, but Sethe and Denver fail to see "the shining" on her, as Paul D calls her seductiveness. Beloved seems simple: she talks little, doesn't know how to do much, acts childishly (except when it comes to Paul D), and needs Denver to keep her occupied. As Paul D moves further and further away from her and, finally, out of the house, she occupies more and more of Denver and Sethe's energy.

At work, Stamp Paid and Paul D are moving pigs toward the slaughter house when Stamp Paid shows him the newspaper article about the murders. Paul D, unable to read, does not know what it says but recognizes the likeness of Sethe. He insists it is not her; the mouth is different. Much to his later regret, Stamp Paid reads the article to Paul D. When Paul D confronts Sethe, she tries to explain that she was saving her children. Paul complains that her kind of loving is too "thick" for him, and he begins to disengage his life from hers, eventually moving out of it for a while.

So involved are the women with Beloved that Denver becomes less sullen and Sethe eventually loses her job for not showing up. Denver knows Sethe cannot take care of them anymore and implores Lady Jones to find her a job, not realizing that jobs are hard to come by and everyone in the community is just about as poor as they are. Unable to offer a job, Lady Jones does make certain the community shares with the family, each different community member leaving some food in their yard at intervals.

By this time, Paul D is living in the basement of the town's storefront church, which horrifies Stamp Paid, who feels that the community should have opened its doors to Paul D, especially since he is a working man willing to pay for his keep. He finds a drinking Paul D on the church steps and apologizes for his neighbors' behavior toward Paul D. He also explains that he was there the day of the murder and it wasn't the way the newspaper said it had been.

Until Denver finds employment, the three women are not doing well—even with their neighbors' sharing. Instead of dividing the food evenly, Sethe gives most of it to Beloved, who is now pregnant with Paul D's child, although Sethe and Denver seem not to know it. Sethe appears to be shrinking, and Denver is losing so much weight that her clothes are too big on her. Besides always being hungry, Sethe is becoming Beloved's slave and complacently abides with her temper tantrums. She is no longer safe from Beloved either, since Beloved apparently attempted to strangle her in Baby Suggs' clearing. After much deliberation, Denver goes to the Bodwins to seek work.

Janey Wagon convinces the Bodwins they need someone to stay with them at night since they are older now and she has her own family to tend. She also spreads the news in the community that Sethe's dead daughter has come back to bedevil her. The women of the community decide to go to 124 Bluestone Road to drive Beloved out. Just as thirty of them gather, Mr. Bodwin arrives to pick up Denver for work. When the women begin to sing, Sethe and Beloved come to the door to see them. Sethe has a confused flashback and thinks Mr. Bodwin is schoolteacher, come to take her children back to slavery. She rushes toward him with the ice pick in her hand as Denver intercedes to save him by leading some others in wrestling her mother down so that Ella may hit her on the jaw. Mr. Bodwin is unaware of the attempt on his life, aware only of the beautiful, naked, pregnant woman standing in the doorway and what he thinks is Sethe going to stop some of the other women from fighting amongst themselves.

Paul D and Denver run into each other on the street. She is still working for the Bodwins, and Miss Bodwin is teaching her. Beloved disappeared the day her mother tried to kill Mr. Bodwin. Sethe is not doing well. Soon, Paul D resumes his residence in Sethe's house. He tries to convince Sethe that she, not Beloved, is her own best thing.

Estimated Reading Time

Because of the constant shift from past to present and back again and the rich metaphoric language which does not state—but rather implies—this is not a quick novel to read despite its moderate length. Rather than rush through it and miss all the visual images, it is suggested you read it in ten sittings, totaling approximately eight hours.

Part One will take half this time with the following breakdown:

- pages 3–42—one hour
- pages 43–85—one hour
- pages 86–113—45 minutes
- pages 114–147—45 minutes
- pages 148–165—half an hour

Part Two will take two and a half hours:

- pages 169–199—one hour
- pages 200–217—45 minutes
- pages 218–235—also 45 minutes

Part Three will need the remaining hour and a half:

- pages 236–262—one hour
- pages 263–275—half an hour

These page numbers are based on the softcover edition of the novel (Morrison, Toni. *Beloved*. New York: Plume Books, 1988). Please remember this is simply an estimation; reading speeds are different for individual readers and some may prefer to dwell on certain parts of the novel while others may choose different sections of the novel in which to invest their time.

Beloved–Part One

Pages 1–19

New Characters:

Sethe: *the protagonist of the novel*

Denver: *Sethe's almost 19-year-old, somewhat simple, daughter who lives with her in isolation at 124 Bluestone Road, the house that had originally been rented, unhaunted, to Baby Suggs*

Paul D: *a former slave who was at Sweet Home in Kentucky with Sethe 18 years earlier*

Baby Suggs: *bought out of slavery at the age of 60 by her son, Halle, who is Sethe's husband; spent many years in her bed deciding whether or not to die*

The Garners: *husband and wife who own Sweet Home; they treat their slaves with a modicum of respect*

schoolteacher: *Mr. Garner's educated brother-in-law who comes to Sweet Home at Mrs. Garner's request to manage the farm and the slaves after Mr. Garner's death*

schoolteacher's nephews: *possibly his sons, it is not made clear which they are; Sethe's attackers while she was nursing and pregnant*

Howard and Buglar: *Sethe's sons; each one runs away as he reaches his teens, fearing the spirit that lives in the house*

Summary

Sethe and Denver have lived alone since Baby Suggs' death almost nine years earlier, right after Howard and Buglar—Sethe's sons and Denver's older brothers—had run away from the spirit that haunts the house within two months of each other. The spirit is thought to be that of Sethe's daughter (born two years before Denver), who died.

Paul D, another former slave from Sweet Home, comes to Sethe's home. As he enters, the spirit makes an appearance as a red light. Paul D thinks it is evil, but Sethe insists it is only sad and full of grief. Sethe tells Paul D how schoolteacher's nephews stole her breast milk, of her whipping, of the birth of Denver as she was fleeing from slavery, and of Baby Suggs' death. The spirit appears again to shake the floorboards of the house, but Paul D sends it away, thereby leaving Denver lonely. They decide that Paul D will stay, Denver's hostility toward him for sending away her only company notwithstanding.

Analysis

These few pages are so chock-full of important events and history in each of the characters' lives that the characters need to be separated from their parts in each others' lives before we may begin to understand them. It is very clear that each has suffered tremendously, and it may be difficult for the reader to assimilate the intricate interweavings of their sorrows. For Sethe, it is the vivid memories of the theft of her breast milk and her whipping. Paul D has never come to terms with having his brother sold away from Sweet Home. Denver suffers in a world of isolation, shunned by the community for something her mother had done. She is lonely and weary of being lonely. Baby Suggs, a spiritual leader of the community, had refused to deal with the world anymore after having had to give away all of her eight babies but one, and now having no idea what had happened to that one. She had taken all the world had given her—slavery until the age of 60 and freedom when her son, Halle bought it—and chose not to take anymore, but rather spend her time in bed concentrating on colors until she died.

But there are pleasant memories here, too. Sethe fondly remembers her careful and courteous treatment by the male slaves

at Sweet Home and joyfully recounts the story of her "bedding" dress to her surviving daughter, Denver. The very name, Beloved, tells us of a slave couple's feeling for their first-born child despite the circumstances into which she is born. These memories became part of the present when Beloved's spirit appears, first as a non-material spirit, then as a material embodiment. There is a blending of the past and the present in that memories are brought forward to become an extant part of the present. Actually, it is the memory of Beloved (as her spirit) which greets Paul D when he first enters the house.

Study Questions

1. Why had Buglar and Howard run away from home?

2. How had Sethe bartered for the lettering on Beloved's head-stone?

3. How had Sethe's children escaped from slavery?

4. Who had been the inhabitants of Sweet Home?

5. Why had Sethe chosen Halle from all the Sweet Home male slaves?

6. Why is Denver so shy?

7. Why do Sethe and Denver argue?

8. What does Sethe tell Paul D about the spirit in the house and the tree on her back?

9. How does Paul D fight the spirit?

10. Why does Denver resent Paul D for having rid the house of the spirit?

Answers

1. Buglar and Howard each had run away from home when he was in his teens, within two months of each other and just prior to Baby Suggs' death when Denver was 10. They had been scared away by the spirit of their dead younger sister. Buglar left when just looking in a mirror caused it to shatter, and Howard left after watching two tiny handprints appear in a cake.

2. Sethe had bartered for the lettering on Beloved's headstone by having sex with the engraver in the graveyard, leaning against the pink, glittery headstone she had chosen for her daughter while his young son watched. The engraver had offered the engraving for free if Sethe would have sex with him for ten minutes. She had then chosen the word/name "Beloved" for the headstone wondering, too late, if she could have had "Dearly" on the headstone if she had offered the engraver an additional ten minutes of sex.

3. Sethe, pregnant for the fourth time, had sent her children from slavery in Kentucky to freedom in Ohio via the Underground Railroad, in a wagon-load of children which had been part of a caravan crossing the river. Once they crossed the river they went to a small town near Cincinnati where their grandmother, Baby Suggs, lived.

4. The inhabitants of Sweet Home had been as follows: Sethe, purchased to replace Baby Suggs when Halle bought her freedom, was the only female slave; Paul F who was sold to meet expenses when Mr. Garner died; Paul D; Halle (Sethe's husband); Sixo; and Paul A. Originally, Mr. and Mrs. Garner were the only whites who lived there but, after Mr. Garner's death, Mrs. Garner invited schoolteacher and his two nephews to live there and manage the farm.

5. After Sethe had been purchased, the male slaves decided to wait, however impatiently and uncomfortably, for her to make her choice among them. It is possible that she had been so impressed with the twenty-year-old Halle's giving up five years of Sundays to buy his mother's freedom that she chose him for that reason.

6. Denver is so shy because she is not used to visitors, not having had any for the past twelve years. She hasn't paid any visits in that long, either.

7. Sethe and Denver have words because Denver is rude to Paul D, asking why they keep talking about Sweet Home when it wasn't either word in its name and then snidely suggesting he spend the night there talking about Sweet Home.

8. Sethe tells Paul D the spirit is that of her daughter who died at the age of two—Denver's older sister—but doesn't mention how or why the child died. She explained that the tree growing on her back is really the scars from the whipping she received from schoolteacher.

9. Paul D fights the spirit by grabbing two legs of the table and bashing it all about, smashing everything and screaming at the spirit to come out and fight him, not Sethe, if it wanted a fight.

10. Denver resents Paul D for having rid the house of the spirit because it's been her only friend for the past twelve years.

Suggested Essay Topics

1. Beloved has an unusual name, but one that says a great deal about her parent's feeling about her birth. As a slave, what justification could Sethe have for giving her firstborn child this name?

2. Baby Suggs feels she leads a life of good fortune, despite having been a slave for sixty years. Pretending you are her, defend and explain what you consider your good fortune.

3. How had Denver's lack of companionship for so many of her developmental years affected her emotional growth? Find specific references in the text to support your opinion.

Pages 20–42

New Characters:

Sixo: *a male slave from Sweet Home who had not allowed slavery to dominate his soul and who was in love with Thirty-Mile Woman*

Amy Denver: *the white, runaway, indentured servant who had helped Sethe as she gave birth to her second daughter while fleeing slavery*

Lu: *the name Sethe had used instead of her own with Amy*

schoolteacher and his nephews: *Mr. Garner's educated brother-in-law, who had come to Sweet Home at Mrs. Garner's request to manage the farm after Mr. Garner's death. He had brought his two nephew with him.*

Thirty-Mile Woman: *Sixo's love and the mother of his unborn child*

Summary

Sethe and Paul D retire to the upstairs bedroom, unable to wait to fully undress one another before they make love. As they wake afterward, Sethe is aware that Paul D is different from Halle, who felt almost like a brother to her since they only saw each other in daylight one day a week—Sunday—despite being married for six years. Paul D is aware of the differences that 18 years have made in Sethe's body.

Denver tells Sethe of the vision she had while peeking in the window. Sethe knelt, and next to her, so did a white dress with its arm around her waist. They ascertain it was not the dress Sethe made herself from remnants for her "bedding" to Halle and decide it must be a symbol for the spirit's coming plans. Sethe remembers this discussion as she thinks of the future with Paul D.

Sethe also tells Paul D a little more of her past: specifically, that schoolteacher came to reclaim her and the children, but she chose to go to jail rather than return to Sweet Home. Because Denver was only a month-old infant, she accompanied her mother to jail. Sethe and Paul D decide he will stay, despite Denver's hostility toward him.

Analysis

The ease with which Sethe and Paul D come together again after so long seems to be a result of their common history or memories. Their manner with each other now is as it was then, with one difference: as far as they know, Sethe is no longer the wife of Paul D's friend. The comfort between them is such that they are willing to deal with Denver's disapproval.

During the intervening years, Paul D had suppressed the part

of himself that would have made living under the horrendous circumstances he encountered unbearable. At the first sight of Sethe, he begins to feel that part of him—his emotions—come alive again. He is a mature man. He sees the undesirable parts of Sethe's body, does not like them, but accepts that the floppy breasts and scarred back are part of her history, of who she is now. She, in her turn, is distrustful of men but something in him (perhaps the part of him that came alive again at the sight of her) is reassuring to her. Denver, the only "fly in the ointment," resents him for not only sending away her only friend, the spirit, but also for making a twosome with her mother—a position only she had filled for the past twelve years.

In addition to Ms. Morrison's blending of the past (via memories) and the present, she blends the present with the future via foreshadowing. The reference to "anything dead coming back" gives us a hint that this will happen. Although the thought is Amy's when she rubs Sethe's feet, we already know Beloved will die soon after Denver's birth and that her spirit is haunting the house Sethe rents from the Bodwins. The subtlety of the foreshadowing only serves to make it more effective.

Study Questions

1. Who was Thirty-Mile Woman?

2. Why didn't Baby Suggs have her children with her?

3. How had Amy helped Sethe?

4. How would you describe the dress Denver sees kneeling next to her mother with its sleeve around her mother's waist?

5. What does Sethe remember of her childhood?

6. According to Sethe, what is "rememory"?

7. Why had Baby Suggs been so starved for color?

8. What is Denver's secret place?

9. What is Paul D's secret fear?

10. What originally caused him to tremble?

Answers

1. Thirty-Mile Woman was the woman Sixo loved. She had lived thirty miles away from Sweet Home, hence, the name. He had tried to walk to her and back in one night. When he realized the walking took all the time he had, he'd found a place halfway and coaxed her to meet him there. Because she had waited in the wrong place and it took time to locate her, he'd simulated a snake bite on her leg so she would not be beaten for being late.

2. Baby Suggs was a slave who bore eight children with six different fathers. The children were constantly being sold. She had no opportunity to say good-bye to her two daughters before hearing of their being sold. She had made an arrangement with the straw boss that she would sleep with him for four months and he would allow her to keep her third child, a son. When she became pregnant with the straw boss' baby, he sold the son he had promised not to. Halle was the only child she was allowed to keep and he had been missing for the last years of her life.

3. Amy had discovered Sethe, just about ready to give birth, laying where she had fallen. Amy had convinced her to crawl to a nearby lean-to. There, Amy had massaged Sethe's swollen feet and legs, bringing some life back to them.

4. The dress Denver sees is high-necked and made of white cotton lisle, with a bustle and buttons all the way down the back.

5. Of her childhood, Sethe remembers song and dance. She remembers her mother, when pointed out to her, wearing a cloth hat rather than the usual straw one. And she remembers the short, curt instruction given to her by the slave who minded the slave children.

6. According to Sethe, "rememory" is a thought picture that people can share rather than a memory that belongs to only those involved in the occasion. It is always there and sometimes people who have nothing to do with it bump into it, sharing it.

7. Baby Suggs had been so starved for color because, except for the two orange squares in a quilt in her room, there was none in the house at 124 Bluestone Road.

8. Denver's secret place is a room created by boxwood bushes, which had been planted in a circular pattern. It is hidden by oak trees between the woods and the stream, beyond the field that lay behind her home.

9. Paul D's secret fear is that he couldn't live with a woman, abide in any one place, for a long period of time.

10. Paul D's trembling was originally caused by being put in an underground box each night that he was in prison.

Suggested Essay Topics

1. Despite (or perhaps due to) being slaves there, Sethe and the male slaves shared a certain kind of fellowship at Sweet Home. Use the novel to find examples of fellowship to validate this statement.

2. Often, that which we hold dear relates more to the symbolism of the object rather than the actual object. How is this true for Amy's admiration of velvet?

3. Baby Suggs talks about a son being more special than just a man. In your opinion, what does she mean by this and how can you prove this from Halle's treatment of her?

Pages 43–64

New Characters:

Beloved: *a young, well-dressed, apparently ill, black woman with soft hands and feet who appears near 124 Bluestone Road unable to remember more than her name*

Here Boy: *Sethe's family dog who refused to enter the house once the haunting began and who disappears when Beloved appears*

Nan: *the one-armed slave who minded the slave children and cooked wherever it was that Sethe had been before Sweet Home*

Summary

Denver snidely asks Paul D how long he'll be "hanging around." Her attitude promotes an argument between Denver and Sethe about Denver's lack of manners and then another between Sethe and Paul D about whether or not she wants him to stay. After he explains that Sethe will not be abandoning Denver by allowing him to stay, they decide that he will stay.

The next day, Paul D takes them to Colored Tuesday at the carnival and succeeds in winning over both the women. When they return home, they find Beloved sleeping on the tree stump near the house. As soon as they see her, Sethe has an overwhelming need to urinate copiously. They can learn only Beloved's name from her but it is clear she is ill. After four glasses of water, Paul D leads her to Baby Suggs' bed, where she sleeps for four days. Since it was common in post-Civil War days for ex-slaves to have secrets they were not ready to share, no questions were asked of strangers, but they were expected to offer their information when they felt it was safe. Denver, suddenly compassionate, takes total charge of the stranger. Paul D becomes suspicious when Beloved shows no inclination to leave nor talk about her life.

After recovering, Beloved becomes attached to Sethe, which flatters Sethe. Beloved begins to ask Sethe questions about things in Sethe's past she could not possibly know about unless she had been there. Sethe tells her stories about Sethe's earlier life; since they do not include the baby, Beloved does not like them.

Analysis

Denver, acting much younger than her years, tries to protect the exclusive relationship she has with Sethe since she feels that is all she has left because Paul D has sent the spirit away. She is easily, childishly, won over by a good time. Sethe, nursing her own doubts, sees the shadow that Paul D, Denver, and she cast—which looks as if they were holding hands—as a sign that there is hope for them.

Only Paul D, who took seven years to walk to Sethe's front door, simply enjoys himself that day for the pure sake of enjoyment. Once they return home, it is as if Paul D were already ensconced in the family: it is he who brings Beloved in for a drink; it is he who suggests she sleep there; and it is he who becomes suspicious when she show no inclination to leave after her recovery.

Beloved has come from water to be reborn and Sethe obliges by urinating copiously when she sees Beloved. While she does not actually give birth here, the urination is very close to the act of voiding the amniotic fluid from the womb just prior to birth. In addition, while neither Sethe nor Denver has left their home for years—other than for Sethe to go to work—they now come out into the community for the carnival at Paul D's insistence. This is similar to a "coach" assisting in bringing the baby into the world during natural childbirth by urging the mother and baby on and helps the baby come out of its comfortable, safe place. The community-at-large responds to this joyous occasion with warm smiles, freely given for the first time in all those years, just as anyone would at a birth.

Study Questions

1. Why does Paul D object to Sethe's apologizing for Denver's behavior toward him?

2. Why does Sethe say she would choose Denver over Paul D if it came to that?

3. How does Beloved get to the stump near 124 Bluestone Road?

4. Why doesn't Paul D press Beloved for more information after she gives her name?

5. What indications do we have that Beloved has become attached to Sethe?

6. How had Sethe obtained her crystal earrings?

7. Why had Sethe made her own "bedding" dress?

8. What materials did Sethe use to make the dress?

9. What does Sethe remember about her mother?

10. What had Nan told Sethe about her mother?

Answers

1. Paul D objects to Sethe apologizing to him for Denver's behavior because he feels Denver is a grown woman and another can't apologize for her. He wants Sethe to treat Denver as a grown woman.

2. Sethe says she would chose Denver over Paul D if it came to that because Denver is her child, no matter how old, and she feels a mother must always protect her child.

3. Beloved gets to the stump near 124 Bluestone Road by walking out of the stream behind the woods, resting that day and night, then spending the next day going through the woods to the field and eventually into the yard.

4. Paul D doesn't press Beloved for more information after she gives her name because so many blacks were running from some kind of trouble after the end of the Civil War that he thought if she wanted them to know her situation, she would tell them without being asked.

5. The indications that Beloved has attached herself to Sethe are that she follows her with her eyes, hovers near Sethe if allowed to, and comes further and further up the road to meet Sethe at the end of her workday as she (Beloved) regains her strength.

6. Sethe had obtained her crystal earrings as a "bedding" present from her owner, Mrs. Garner, when she chose Halle and asked for a wedding—a request Mrs. Garner had ignored.

7. Sethe had made her own "bedding" dress because she was disappointed not to be having a wedding with a ceremony, a preacher, and a party. She felt she should at least have the dress.

8. The "bedding" dress had been made from stolen bits and pieces. The top was two pillow cases stolen from Mrs. Garner's mending basket; a dresser scarf with a candle burn

hole in it was the front of the skirt; one of Mrs. Garner's old sashes scorched by being used to test the flat iron was the sash; and mosquito netting which had been used for straining jelly—then washed and soaked by Sethe—was the back of the skirt.

9. Sethe remembers that her mother, who had been allowed to nurse her for only a few weeks, once showed her the brand she had under her breast, and that she told Sethe she was the only person left alive who had this brand. Her mother was later hanged.

10. Nan revealed that Sethe's mother did not name and threw away the baby she'd had from a white crew member on the ship bringing them to North America and did the same with the babies she'd had with other white men. Sethe is the only baby she'd kept and named.

Suggested Essay Topics

1. Sethe murdered one of her children and attempted to murder the others; her mother threw away all her babies but one. Using the text as reference, explain how mother love can be this strong.

2. Beloved is not pressed for information when she appears, yet is accepted into the household. Referring to specific passages in the novel, contrast Paul D's reason for not asking any questions with those of Sethe and Denver.

3. Sethe and Denver seem to allow Paul D to instantaneously become head of the household once Sethe agrees to allow him to move in. Based on Sethe's prior experiences so far in the novel, how can you rationalize her actions in this matter?

Pages 64–85

New Characters:

Mister: *the rooster from Sweet Home whose egg shell Paul D cracked so that he could live and who now preys on Paul D's mind*

Mr. Buddy: *the possible father, and definite master, of Amy Denver*

Summary

Paul D is wary of Beloved's attentions to him and wants her to leave, but cannot ask her to since it is Sethe's home. As he relentlessly questions her as to how she came to be there, she chokes on a raisin, effectively ending the questioning. She and Denver go to Denver's room, and Paul D tells Sethe that Halle saw schoolteacher's nephew steal her milk, which caused Halle to lose his mind because he could not stop them. He also tells her about his own torture with the bit in his mouth and of having Mister, the rooster he helped hatch, free and watching this humiliation.

Denver believes Beloved is the spirit of her sister returned in the flesh and urges Beloved not to tell Sethe. Denver's advice ends the dancing they have been doing and causes an argument. In an attempt to soothe Beloved, Denver tells her how Amy helped Sethe give birth to Denver.

Analysis

As the story switches from present to past, the divisions between the two become vague. Denver has no difficulty accepting that Beloved is her sister, although her sister had died almost nineteen years earlier. Paul D finds himself telling Sethe of Halle's insanity and his own torture as if it were yesterday, not all those years ago. Sethe, herself, wants only to have gone insane then, too, instead of having spent all these years suffering. Beloved speaks of those years without any references to time. The transition from Denver's telling the story of her birth to Sethe's giving birth to Denver is so suitable that it seems the two have blended and that time has, too. The blending of time in the novel—past, present, and future (while in the past)—is one of Ms. Morrison's most successful literary devices. It effectively allows the reader to be inside the character's mind at all times of the character's life, not just at the moment or in a memory of the moment, as is usually the case in developing a character.

Study Questions

1. Why does Paul D question Beloved so relentlessly?

2. How does the questioning end?

3. Why hadn't Halle helped Sethe when he witnessed the brutality the nephews inflicted on her?

4. Why does Paul D keep remembering Mister in the face of his torture?

5. Why does Sethe wish she had gone insane?

6. How do we know Denver is assured Beloved is the spirit of her sister?

7. How had Amy treated "Lu's" back?

8. How had Amy fashioned shoes for Sethe?

9. Why had Denver been born in a boat?

10. Why had Amy left Sethe after Denver's birth?

Answers

1. Paul D questions Beloved so relentlessly because he wants her to leave. It's been five weeks since her appearance and she is interested in him sexually. He cannot understand why both Sethe and Denver do not see this. Both Beloved's interest in him and the fact that the other women do not see it is disturbing to him.

2. The questioning ends when Beloved chokes on a raisin. Afterward, she is tired and wants to go to bed.

3. Halle hadn't helped Sethe when he witnessed the brutality the nephews inflicted upon her because he knew he, himself, could be subdued and possibly killed if he did. His fail-

ure to come to her aid was so distressing to Halle that he could not accept it and went insane.

4. Paul D keeps remembering Mister in the face of his torture because he had helped this rooster hatch and then he, Paul D, was tortured by man—while the rooster remained the same: a rooster, unchanged by what man could do to him, even in death.

5. Sethe wishes she had gone insane because she is suffering so from Paul D's telling her of her husband's insanity and Paul D's own torture. While she wishes she had had this sweet oblivion, she also knows, as a mother, she could not have done so, for her children needed her.

6. We know Denver is assured that Beloved is the spirit of her sister because she asks Beloved not to reveal her identity to Sethe, and also asks if Beloved remembers playing with Denver by the stream.

7. Amy had treated "Lu's" back with a poultice of cleaned spider-webs in order to draw out the pus in the wounds produced by the whipping.

8. The shoes Amy had made for Sethe were pieces of Sethe's shawl filled with leaves and tied over Sethe's feet.

9. Denver had been born in a boat because Sethe went into hard labor and her amniotic fluid released just as they reached the river. She had seen the boat and headed directly for it.

10. Amy had left Sethe after Denver's birth because she was herself a runaway indentured servant and afraid to be caught, as they would be on this busy river, with a runaway slave.

Suggested Essay Topics

1. In the pain and humiliation of his torture, Paul D focuses on the rooster, Mister, as the symbol of what was wrong in his life. Citing other examples from the novel, explain how people often choose a symbol, rather than an actual event,

upon which to dwell in times of extreme duress.

2. Amy runs away to find velvet, Sethe to better the lives of her children. How are the two women's motives for running similar and dissimilar. Remember: the text is your source.

3. Paul D stops questioning Beloved when she chokes on a raisin. Physical acts are often caused by emotional reactions to a situation. How is this true for both Sethe and Denver, as illustrated by what we know of each of their life's stories so far?

Pages 86–113

New Characters:

Stamp Paid: *an older, ex-slave who is part of the Underground Railroad and ferries Sethe, with the new-born Denver, over the river to freedom*

Ella: *another freed slave, a contemporary of Stamp Paid's, who helps Sethe and Denver once they've crossed the river to freedom and arrive at Baby Suggs' home in Ohio*

Lady Jones: *a light-skinned, free black who runs the children's school that the then seven-year-old Denver attends for a year*

Nelson Lord: *Denver's classmate, who innocently asks her about the murder, Sethe's imprisonment, and Denver's accompanying her mother to jail*

Summary

Sethe feels she needs a ceremony to lay down her burdens and so takes Beloved and Denver with her to The Clearing, where Baby Suggs formerly led her spiritual community. She feels fingers massaging her neck and then choking her. She thinks it is the spirit of the nine-years-dead Baby Suggs, but Denver quietly tells Beloved she knows Beloved did this. While in The Clearing, Sethe remembers her 28 days of freedom (before the murder and after her es-

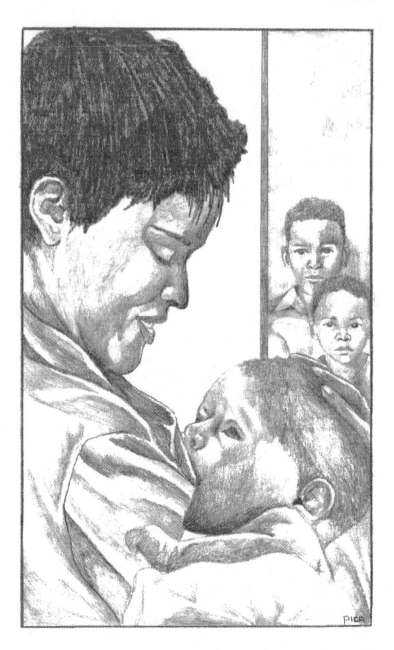

cape from slavery), acknowledges Halle is gone forever, and realizes she does want Paul D in her life.

We learn of Denver's two years of deafness after her classmate, Nelson Lord, innocently asked her about the murder and she, in turn, asked her mother but could not abide to hear the answers. Paul D remembers his imprisonment for the attempted murder of Brandywine, the man to whom schoolteacher sold him, and his escape. He thinks of the 46 men chained together, escaping from a mud slide during the rains and running until they found the Cherokee, who freed them of their shackles. He was the last prisoner to leave them. The Cherokee showed him how to follow the tree blossoms north. He laments "the tobacco tin lodged in his chest" that used to be his heart, and relives the trembling of his body caused by being locked in an underground box each of the 86 nights of his imprisonment in Alfred, Georgia.

Analysis

While Sethe attempts to come to terms with her life as it is now, the spirits are not done with her. She is mystified as to why Baby Suggs, who had been so loving and supportive toward her would try to choke her but accepts what she thinks is the truth of this. She sees her need for Paul D, a man who not only shares her history but one who wants and accepts her. Denver also is accepting: in her case, it is of Beloved as the reembodied spirit of her sister and of Beloved's choking of Sethe. Paul D remembers his prison experience, without effort but with great pain, and feels his heart may still come alive as he felt it start to when he first came upon Sethe in her yard. Only Beloved seems to have no acceptance nor understanding: she is jealous of Paul D's relationship with Sethe, just as she is of the time Sethe spends with Denver. She makes her first physical effort at hurting Sethe, which does not go unnoticed by Denver.

Study Questions

1. Why does Sethe take Denver and Beloved to The Clearing where Baby Suggs formerly led her spiritual community?

2. What happens at The Clearing?

3. How does Denver know it is Beloved, not Baby Suggs, who did this to Sethe?

4. What had Stamp Paid told the boy when he saw Sethe for the first time?

5. What had Sethe done with her 28 days of freedom?

6. How had Baby Suggs greeted Sethe?

7. Why had Denver left the school and become deaf?

8. What had the prison been like for Paul D in Alfred, Georgia?

9. How had the Cherokee helped Paul D?

10. Who was the weaver lady?

Answers

1. Sethe takes Denver and Beloved to The Clearing where Baby Suggs had formerly led her spiritual community because she feels a need for ceremony to lay her burdens down and come to peace with Paul D's living with her and the information he gave her about Halle and his own torture.

2. At The Clearing, Sethe sits on a rock to pray and conjure Baby Suggs' fingers massaging her neck. She succeeds, but the massage turns into choking. Denver ends this by turning her gasping mother over on her back.

3. Denver knows it was Beloved, not Baby Suggs, who choked Sethe because she had been watching Beloved's face.

4. Stamp Paid had told the boy to take off his coat to wrap the newborn baby in. When the boy whined, Stamp Paid told him to take his coat back, but if he could do that, to go away and not return.

5. In her 28 days of freedom, between escaping slavery and being imprisoned for the murder of her daughter, Sethe learned the alphabet and new sewing stitches, healed herself, relaxed, talked with the others, and learned how to be a free person making her own decisions.

6. Baby Suggs had greeted Sethe by kissing her on the mouth

and refusing to let her see the other children until she was cleaned up. She washed Sethe and tended to her feet while another woman tended to the baby. Then she gave Denver to her to nurse. When she discovered the blood on the bed sheets from Sethe's whipping wounds, Baby Suggs greased her back.

7. Nelson Lord, one of the other young students in Lady Jones' school, innocently asked Denver questions about the murder, Sethe's imprisonment, and Denver's imprisonment with her. Denver ran home to ask her mother, but could not hear Sethe. For the next two years, Denver was deaf. She never returned to the school.

8. The prison that Paul D had been in in Alfred, Georgia, was a hell-hole. There were 46 men chained together daily to work on a chain gang and unchained each night to be put into individual boxes buried under the ground. They were guarded by men with rifles and dogs. Their only slight relief was to sing out their pain as they hammered each day.

9. The Cherokee had helped Paul D and the other prisoners by breaking off their shackles and taking the escaped prisoners into their camp. One by one, each of the other prisoners left until only Paul D remained. The Cherokee showed him how to follow the tree blossoms to the north when he decided it was time to leave.

10. The weaver lady was the woman Paul D met when he finally arrived in Delaware. She was kind to him, passing him off as her nephew from Syracuse by calling him by the nephew's name. Paul D stayed with her for 18 months.

Suggested Essay Topics

1. Paul D stayed with the weaver lady for 18 months, not because he loved her nor because of only her kindness, but because she fulfilled very specific needs of his. Often in life, we do as another asks because it does adhere to our own needs. What is it that Paul D was seeking that he found here, and why didn't he stay longer?

2. Sethe's need for a ritual or ceremony is not unusual. What other rituals or ceremonies had Sethe experienced in her life that would have led her to the need for one now in order to lay her burden down?

3. It is difficult for Sethe to accept Paul D's presence in her life, even though this is what she wants. Sometimes, happiness is just as hard to acclimate to as unhappiness. How do you think it will be possible for Sethe to adjust? Validate your opinion with facts from the book.

Pages 114–147

New Characters:

John: *Ella's husband and also a part of the Underground Railroad*

Janey Wagon: *a free black woman who washes and cooks for the Bodwins*

Summary

Paul D is forced out of the house by Beloved. He moves from Sethe's bed to the rocker, from the rocker to Baby Suggs' bed, from Baby Suggs' bed to the storeroom, and finally from the storeroom to the coldhouse. It is in the coldhouse that Beloved succeeds in seducing him over a three-week-period during which he feels his heart come back to life. Denver becomes certain that Beloved was the white dress she saw holding Sethe's waist in the vision she'd had before Beloved's arrival. She feels she must continuously entertain Beloved with stories and songs or Beloved will go back from whence she came.

Paul D doesn't understand why he is having sex with Beloved when he loves Sethe more each day. He decides to meet Sethe after her workday to tell her, but asks her to have his baby instead. She decides, after having brought Paul D back to her bed, that another baby is not a good idea.

In flashback, Baby Suggs remembers the feast for 90 people

that had started with Stamp Paid bringing pail after pail of black berries to her and ending with the community agreeing that she is too "uppity"—which they claimed was caused by her abundance of good fortune.

Analysis

It seems there was no winning for freed slaves. Baby Suggs' community decided she is too "uppity" since she has her daughter-in-law and grandchildren with her and her son had bought her out of slavery, not to mention the Bodwins' two-story house (where she lives) and the abundance of food and good times at the feast. They seem to have forgotten the seven sold children she could not locate despite two years of inquiries, and the daily pain of her hip, which had been broken while doing field work. There is no mention of the husband (who taught her cobbling and gave her his name) she hoped had fled to freedom, nor of her 60 years as a slave before Halle bought her freedom, nor is her spiritual calling, her assistance, or her house being used as a meeting place remembered. She's had these feelings of unease before but they were related to white people, not her own people.

Study Questions

1. Why does Paul D make love to Sethe each morning before he is seduced by Beloved?

2. Why does Denver enjoy Beloved's staring at her?

3. What happens between Denver and Beloved in the cold house?

4. How do Paul D and Sethe conduct themselves when he meets her after work?

5. How does he see her pregnancy as a solution to his problem?

6. Why does Beloved think her body is falling apart?

7. How would you describe the feast at Baby Suggs' house?

8. Why had her congregation shunned Baby Suggs and her family after the feast?

9. Why hadn't Baby Suggs been able to find her children?

10. Why had the Bodwins been so helpful to Baby Suggs?

Answers

1. Paul D makes love to Sethe each morning before he is seduced by Beloved because he knows Beloved seeks him sexually and he wants to have no appetite for her, since it is Sethe he loves more each day.

2. Denver enjoys Beloved's staring at her because she feels Beloved is "interested" and "uncritical." It makes her feel Beloved needs something from her.

3. When Denver and Beloved go to the coldhouse to get the cider, Denver cannot see in the dark and loses Beloved, who seems to magically disappear. She thinks Beloved has returned to wherever it was she came from and is bereft until Beloved shows herself again.

4. Paul D and Sethe conduct themselves like children when he meets her after work: laughing, holding hands, patting each other's behind, hugging, and Paul D giving Sethe a piggyback ride.

5. Paul D sees Sethe's pregnancy, to which she has not agreed nor is yet a reality, as a solution to his problem because it would help him "...hold on to her, document his manhood and break out of the girl's spell—all in one."

6. Beloved thinks her body is falling apart because she's pulled out a back tooth which is rotten. She thinks this is the beginning of her body falling apart, which means the end of this embodiment and her current life.

7. The feast at Baby Suggs' house had consisted of 90 people eating an abundance of blackberry pie, turkey, strawberry smash (punch), perch, cat fish, corn pudding with cream, rabbit, raised bread, shortbread, batter bread, and bread pudding. All were laughing as the tired, overfed children fell asleep in the grass.

8. Baby Suggs' congregation had shunned her and her family after the feast because they felt she was too "uppity": their proof had been that she had a two-story house, the Bodwins had helped her, her daughter-in-law and grandchildren were with her, and she had had an overabundance of food at the feast.

9. Baby Suggs had not been able to find her children once she was free and living at 124 Bluestone Road because the Whitlow place, where the children had been born, was gone and "a man named Dunn" somewhere in the West hadn't been a good enough address for a letter to be delivered.

10. The Bodwins had been helpful to Baby Suggs because they were both anti-slavery and friends of Mr. Garner, her former owner at Sweet Home.

Suggested Essay Topics

1. Although the Garners considered themselves enlightened slave owners, they are still slave owners. Compare and contrast their thoughts on slavery with those of the anti-slavery Bodwins.

2. Paul D's reason for wanting Sethe pregnant with his child is shockingly contemporary. The difference from today's situations is that Sethe is a mature woman who is able to consider the offer in terms of her experience rather than as a love-stricken young girl. What is Sethe's reason for deciding not to have Paul D's baby, and how did she arrive at this decision?

3. Baby Suggs offers a feast for her friends and neighbors. Rather than being thankful after the feast, her friends and neighbors begin to shun her. How much of this shunning do you think is jealousy and how do you explain it? Follow the text closely to explain your reasoning.

Pages 148–165

New Character:

Aunt Phyllis: *the midwife from Minnowville who Mr. Garner sent for each time Sethe gave birth*

Summary

Schoolteacher, one of his nephews (the other having been kept home as punishment for stealing Sethe's milk), and a slave catcher had arrived with the sheriff to capture Sethe and her children. Sethe recognized schoolteacher's hat and had gathered her children in the shed where she beat the boys on the head with a shovel in an attempt to kill them, slit Beloved's throat, and tried to bash Denver's brains out against a wall. Stamp Paid caught Denver and saved her life. Baby Suggs saw that the boys were still breathing and tended to them. Sethe would not loosen her hold on the dead Beloved; therefore, Baby Suggs told her it was time to nurse Denver but they had to trade children in order for Sethe to do so. Sethe and her daughter, nursing from a nipple still covered with Beloved's blood, were taken to prison after the sheriff had sent off schoolteacher, his nephew, and the slave catcher.

Stamp Paid brings a newspaper article to Paul D. It has a picture of a woman who looks remarkably like Sethe, but Paul D keeps insisting the mouth is not right. Stamp Paid tells Paul D about the picnic-barbecue, then reads the article to him since Paul D cannot read. Paul D goes home to Sethe to ask her about the veracity of the newspaper article. Instead of answering him, she spins in a circle and tells rambling stories. Finally, she explains that she had to make her children safe from slavery and their deaths were the only way she could achieve their safety. Paul D argues with her as to whether or not her plan succeeded and leaves.

Analysis

While Paul D understands how being free gives you permission to love in a big way rather than the fearful, minimal way slaves have been taught to love, he cannot accept that this love—grown

to its fullest in freedom—gives the right to kill, even if you think it's keeping the object of your love safe. He suggests to Sethe that this was the action of an animal, not a human, and it didn't work: Beloved is dead, both Buglar and Howard ran away, and Denver is seemingly a dim-witted, dependent child. Sethe, for her part, cannot agree with him; she'd lived in slavery and felt that was worse than death for her children. She had killed out of love, not rage or punishment.

Study Questions

1. Why hadn't Baby Suggs been warned of the slave catchers' approach by her community?

2. Why had Sethe taken her children to the shed as soon as she recognized schoolteacher's hat?

3. How had Stamp Paid saved Denver's life?

4. Why had the sheriff sent schoolteacher, his nephew, and the slave catcher away?

5. How had Baby Suggs been able to take Beloved's body from Sethe after Stamp Paid had been unsuccessful at this?

6. Why had Denver been taken prisoner with her mother?

7. Why does Stamp Paid show Paul D the newspaper article?

8. Why does Paul D keep insisting the mouth of the woman in the picture with the newspaper article is not Sethe's?

9. How does Sethe react when Paul D confronts her with the events reported in the newspaper article?

10. Why does she think Paul D is not coming back when he leaves?

Answers

1. Baby Suggs hadn't been warned of the slave catcher's approach by her community because they had been shunning her for "uppityness" since the day of the picnic–barbecue.

2. Sethe had taken her children to the shed as soon as she rec-

ognized schoolteacher's hat in order to kill them, rather than allow them to be returned to slavery.

3. Stamp Paid saved Denver's life by snatching her from her mother's grasp as Sethe swung her against the wall a second time, having missed the first, in an attempt to bash out her brains.

4. The sheriff had sent schoolteacher, his nephew, and the slave catcher away because they were no longer needed. The children could not be returned to Sweet Home because one was still nursing, one dead, and the other two were now incapable of doing the work awaiting them there. The sheriff, himself, had to arrest Sethe for murder.

5. Baby Suggs had been able to take Beloved's body from Sethe after Stamp Paid had tried unsuccessfully by tricking her. She had told Sethe it was time to nurse Denver but that she had to deal with one child at a time. Sethe complied and let go of Beloved.

6. Denver had been taken to prison with her mother because she was still a nursing infant and needed her mother's milk, despite the fact that she was already almost crawling.

7. Stamp Paid shows Paul D the newspaper article because it was clear that Paul D had no inkling of the event it reported and Stamp Paid felt Paul D should know.

8. Paul D keeps insisting the mouth of the woman in the picture with the newspaper article is not Sethe's because he does not want to hear the bad news that goes along with a black face being in the newspaper. After hearing the article, he does not want to believe Sethe is guilty of the murder and attempted murders.

9. When Paul D confronts Sethe with the events reported in the newspaper article, she begins spinning around the room and tells him rambling stories without answering until he forces her to answer by not smiling.

10. Sethe thinks Paul D is not coming back when he leaves be-

cause he had inferred she was an animal to do this to her children in the name of keeping them safe. After he said this, she felt the distance between them. He is also careful not to say "good-bye," as if she were somehow too fragile to cope with the realization that he is leaving.

Suggested Essay Topics

1. Compare Baby Suggs' treatment at the hands of her masters in slavery with her treatment by her community as a free woman. Document your thoughts with examples from the text.

2. Sixo had never allowed his spirit to be enslaved, even though his body was. Agree or disagree with this statement being certain to use facts from the novel to support your argument.

3. Explain how you may, or may not, use Denver's suckling her sister's blood along with her mother's milk (directly after Beloved's murder) in accounting for both her acceptance of the non-material spirit in the house and her acceptance of Beloved as the material re-embodiment of her sister's spirit.

SECTION THREE

Beloved–Part Two

Pages 169–199

New Characters:

Mr. Bodwin: *the brother of Miss Bodwin, also an anti-slavery white person who does whatever he can to help with the Underground Railroad and the newly-liberated slaves*

Reverend Pike: *the reverend of the store-front church where Paul D is living in the basement, also the religious leader who conducted the funerals for both Beloved and Baby Suggs*

Sawyer: *Sethe's employer at the restaurant*

Summary

Stamp Paid, remorseful for having read the newspaper article to Paul D, and now worried about Sethe's well-being, goes to 124 Bluestone Road for the first time since Baby Suggs' death. He has a hard time getting himself to knock instead of just walking in as he's used to doing in the community. His knock is not answered although he hears voices, so he looks in the window and sees the girls. He recognizes Denver, but not Beloved, and decides to make inquiries about her. Six times in as many days he tries to force himself to knock on the door, but simply can't.

Beloved finds a pair of ice skates. Sethe searches the house and finds one half of another pair. The three women have an uproari-

ous time skating on the lake. Sethe's laughter turns to uncontrollable weeping, but the girls are not immediately aware of the change in her emotions nor her lack of control over her emotions. They return to the house to warm up and Beloved begins humming a song she couldn't have known, since Sethe had made it up for her children when they were small.

Sethe begins not to care for the outside world. She is late for work for the first time in sixteen years and begins locking the door to her home. She is convinced that Beloved is her daughter come back to her and, since Beloved is back, her sons will also return. Meanwhile, Stamp Paid goes to John and Ella to find out who the girl is. Ella doesn't know but, by way of telling him to ask Paul D, mentions that Paul D is sleeping in the basement of the church, which outrages Stamp Paid's sense of honor for the community.

Analysis

Sethe is closing off her world. Her husband is missing, possibly dead, certainly insane. Baby Suggs is dead. Her sons have run away. Paul D has come and enriched her life, but—like everyone else—has left. Beloved knows things she cannot know unless she was there, years ago, when the children were small. Sethe chooses to make her world consist of Beloved, Denver, and herself.

Although the decision seems to be impulsive—when she hears the song Beloved is humming—the process is slow. She is late for work for the first time; she begins to lock the door; she decides not to trust any white folk—even Mr. Bodwin, who had seen the judge in chambers before her murder trial to plead for her life.

The song seems to be the last straw in a large straw pile, rather than the one act that makes her decide, just as losing Paul D after their love is another straw in that pile.

Sethe has encountered more in her life than a human being should have to deal with, as she'd lamented when Paul D told her Halle saw schoolteacher's nephews brutalize her, and now there seems to be no choice: if she cannot go insane, she'll have to close off the rest of the world, which can't be trusted anyway.

Study Questions

1. How had the community conducted itself when Baby Suggs died?

2. Why wasn't Stamp Paid used to knocking on the doors of the community?

3. What are Sethe, Denver, and Beloved doing when Beloved begins to hum the song she couldn't know?

4. Why does Stamp Paid suddenly understand Baby Suggs' indifference to the world once she'd decided to die?

5. What does Sethe realize about the shadows she had seen at the carnival?

6. What does Sethe remember of the efforts to save her life?

7. Why is Stamp Paid outraged when Ella tells him that Paul D is sleeping in the basement of the church?

8. Why does Sethe pilfer from Sawyer?

9. Why had Sethe asked Mrs. Garner what "characteristics" meant?

10. How had Mr. Garner died?

Answers

1. When Baby Suggs died, the community set up the funeral meal in the yard because no one wanted to enter 124 Bluestone Road. Sethe retaliated by refusing their food and not joining the service, standing apart near the grave instead.

2. Stamp Paid wasn't used to knocking on the doors of the community because they were always open to him, as if they were his own, in payment for all his services in the Underground Railroad—bringing messages back and forth, providing food, spreading news that needed spreading, and getting whatever was needed to the person who needed it as soon as possible.

3. Sethe, Denver, and Beloved are drinking hot, sweet milk in an effort to warm up and calm down from the skating expedition when Beloved begins to hum a song that she couldn't

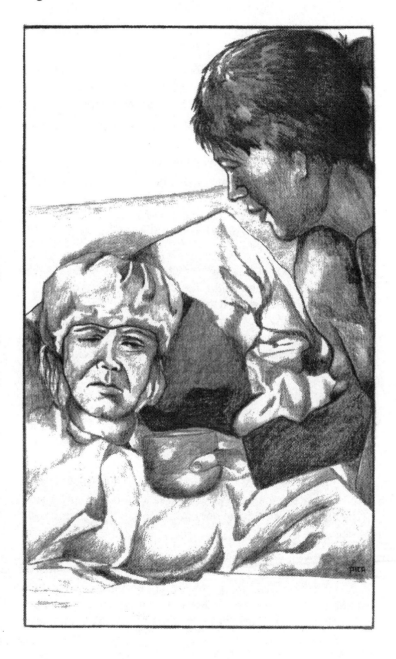

know because Sethe had made it up for her children when they were small.

4. Stamp Paid suddenly understands Baby Suggs' indifference to the world once she'd decided to die because he, himself, is tired: not just bone-weary, but marrow-weary.

5. Sethe realizes the three hand-holding shadows behind them at the carnival were not those of Sethe, Denver, and Paul D as she had thought, but of Sethe, Denver, and Beloved.

6. Sethe remembers that, in an effort to save her life, Mr. Bodwin had seen the judge in his chambers and the Colored Ladies of Delaware circulated a petition. She also remembers the two white preachers and the newspaperman who had come to see her.

7. Stamp Paid is outraged when Ella tells him Paul D is sleeping in the basement of the church because it isn't charitable not to have offered him better accommodations, even without his asking. He thinks the community is now ostracizing Paul D because of his association with Sethe, just as it has ostracized her all these years because of her association with Baby Suggs.

8. Sethe pilfers from Sawyer because she doesn't want the humiliation of having to wait in line at the back door of Phelps Store, with the people who want nothing to do with her, while Phelps waits on all the white people before he comes to the back door.

9. Sethe had asked Mrs. Garner what "characteristics" meant because she inadvertently heard schoolteacher tell his students to make a list of her human and animal characteristics.

10. According to Mrs. Garner, Mr. Garner had died of an exploded ear drum caused by a stroke; however, Sixo had said the hole was caused by a bullet shot by a jealous neighbor. Schoolteacher then took the guns away from the slaves which leads one to believe that Mr. Garner's death may have been murder.

Suggested Essay Topics

1. Only Sixo believes Mr. Garner's death was a murder, yet schoolteacher takes the guns away from the slaves once he hears what Sixo has to say. What might have motivated schoolteacher to take the guns if he does not accept Sixo's theory?

2. Stamp Paid reads the newspaper article about Sethe to Paul D in an attempt to protect him from future unhappiness, yet Paul D is very unhappy once he hears what the article says. How can you rationalize Stamp Paid's intention in reading Paul D the article?

3. Sethe begins to hide herself in the tiny world of her home and yard once again. Track the events that lead her to decide upon this seclusion and explain how each step could seem a logical progression to Sethe.

Pages 200–217

Summary

Sethe comes to the conclusion that Beloved is the embodiment of her murdered daughter who had no choice but to come back in the flesh since Paul D drove her non-material spirit out. She suspects Baby Suggs helped her return. She thinks over the scratches on Beloved's forehead and sees them as her own fingernail prints from where she had held Beloved's head back in order to slit her throat and remembers she had wanted to die when she put up Beloved's gravestone, but couldn't—she had other children to care for.

Denver had been afraid of Sethe ever since she can remember, feeling safe only in Grandma Suggs' room at night. Her brothers, before they left, kept telling her how to kill Sethe if Sethe tried to kill her as she had Beloved. Except for Baby Suggs' funeral and the day at the carnival, Denver has not left the house nor the yard since going deaf at the age of seven when she had asked Sethe if what Nelson Lord said about the murders and imprisonment was true. She feels she must keep Beloved safe from Sethe this time because Halle will be coming for them.

Beloved describes her journey back to the flesh after existing as the spirit that haunted 124 Bluestone Road and mentions Sethe's earrings several times. She remembers three frustrations: first, the clouds of gun smoke which blinded her and prevented her from following Sethe; second, when Sethe jumped into the sea instead of smiling at Beloved; and third, under the bridge when she went to join Sethe but, while Sethe came toward her, she did not smile. Beloved has found Sethe now, in this house, smiling.

Analysis

This is the most complex section of this novel that we've dealt with so far. The three women's "rememories" are interwoven, but it is becoming clear which memory is whose. Sethe is clearly delighted that her daughter is back, forgives her mother, and will stay forever. Denver has lived in fear her whole life and still feels she must protect herself and her sister, whose non-material spirit was HER secret until Paul D came. Beloved feels whole, reunited (with both her mother and her sister), and greedy for love—seemingly more than either woman can give her, although both her sister and her mother each call Beloved "mine." When the women speak together, they affirm that Beloved will no longer leave and that Sethe and Denver will take care of her.

Part of what makes this section so complex is that Beloved moves easily from discussing her actions as a non-material spirit to discussing those performed while a spirit in the flesh. Sethe and Denver seem to have no difficulty accepting her two states (non-material spirit, then spirit in the flesh or material re-embodiment), but it may be too intricate for a reader to quickly comprehend. Add this to the stream-of-consciousness writing technique—without punctuation—and it becomes necessary to remind the reader to flow with the words rather than stopping where one would ordinarily expect a sentence or a thought to end. It is this "flow" that allows the women to speak simultaneously, and concurrently maintain their individuality.

Study Questions

1. Why had Sethe stuttered until she met Halle?

2. How had Denver drunk her sister's blood?

3. Why had Denver kept pretending to love Sethe?

4. How had Halle tried to make his mother more comfortable?

5. How had Baby Suggs viewed Denver?

6. Why had the "men without skins" given the Negroes their urine?

7. How was Beloved able to find the house?

8. What does Beloved admit to Sethe?

9. What warning does Denver give Beloved?

10. What accusation does Beloved make of Sethe?

Answers

1. Sethe stuttered until she met Halle as a result of having seen her mother's body when she was lynched. Sethe wanted to look for the brand underneath her mother's breast, but Nan had pulled her away.

2. Denver drank her sister's blood directly after Sethe murdered Beloved, whose blood covered Sethe. In order to get Beloved's body from Sethe, Baby Suggs had told her it was time to nurse Denver and that they needed to trade children. Sethe had refused to clean herself first, so Denver ended up suckling Beloved's blood, which was on Sethe's nipple, along with Sethe's milk.

3. Denver kept pretending to love Sethe because she was terrified Sethe would murder her, too. She had nightmares about it and her brothers had repeatedly given her ways to kill Sethe if she had to after they left.

4. Halle tried to make his mother more comfortable by devising a pulley for her to use to raise herself off the floor after sleeping and made a step for her so that her body would be level when she was standing.

5. Baby Suggs viewed Denver as charmed since she had been saved when her sister was murdered and her brothers almost murdered.

6. The "men without skins"—white people—had given the Negroes their urine because there was no water. The Negroes had so little water in their bodies that they could neither cry nor urinate and would surely die if their water levels were not replenished.

7. Beloved was able to find the house because Sethe told her where it was.

8. Beloved admits to Sethe that she is, indeed, the spirit of Beloved, come back to life in this body.

9. Denver warns Beloved to beware of loving Sethe too much because she can give Beloved nightmares.

10. Beloved accuses Sethe of letting one of the "men without skin" hurt her.

Suggested Essay Topics

1. Denver says she has been afraid of Sethe for as long as she can remember. Using the text as your source, document and explain her fear. Be certain to include her brothers' advice and her own actions to protect Beloved.

2. Some say that adversity makes the bonds between people stronger. How could you prove, or disprove, this for Beloved and Denver, starting at the beginning of the adversity they faced, when Denver inadvertently drank Beloved's blood?

3. Halle had been an excellent son, a good husband, and a good father, yet he was insane the last time Paul D saw him. Compare and contrast the views of him held by his mother, his wife, his friend, and his daughters.

Pages 218–235

New Characters:

Vashti: *Stamp Paid's now-deceased wife*

Joshua: *Stamp Paid's former slave name*

Summary

Paul D is drinking on the steps of the church, remembering when Stamp Paid finds him in order to apologize for no one in the community offering to take him in (Paul D tells him Reverend Pike offered, but he preferred to be alone), and to tell him he, Stamp Paid, had been present when Sethe killed Beloved and tried to kill her other children. He tells Paul D it wasn't like he thinks it was. Paul D is full of his own thoughts about the past: the attempted escape from Sweet Home; Sixo being burned and shot; Halle going insane; Paul A being missing; Thirty-Mile Woman—pregnant with Sixo's child—being sent running by Sixo when it was clear they were going to be caught; not knowing his father; not remembering his mother; his own torture; and the way his heart stopped when Sethe had told him she'd already sent the children ahead and was going to run herself.

Then Stamp Paid tells Paul D how he renamed himself, how his wife Vashti had to sleep with the young master, and how frustrating it had been to Stamp Paid that he could neither kill the young master nor break Vashti's neck. He asks about Beloved, and together they figure out she is probably the young girl who had been locked up in a house with a white man all winter. When spring came, the man was dead and the girl gone.

Analysis

Paul D sees nothing in his life but losses and empty spaces until he thinks about Sethe. But he thinks of her as a loss too, regretting the fact that his "tobacco tin" (heart) has been unlocked by her after so long, only to be left blowing in the wind. He is very aware that he has no family history, no family present, and from the looks of it now, no family future. He is in mourning for what could have

been and beseeches Stamp Paid to tell him just how much a man is supposed to take.

Stamp Paid, in explaining why he renamed himself, reveals his own sorrows: being a murderous husband who cannot kill either the young master soiling his wife nor the wife forced into this coupling, his throwing himself into helping the community only to find it torn apart by jealousy supposedly caused by "uppityness," and his marrow-deep bone weariness. Neither man—Paul D protesting nor Stamp Paid accepting—sees a way out of misery.

Study Questions

1. How had schoolteacher changed life at Sweet Home?

2. What had been their plan for escape from slavery?

3. Why hadn't Thirty-Mile Woman been caught?

4. Why had Sixo been burned and then shot to death?

5. How had Paul D been tortured when he was captured?

6. What does the white stranger tell the two men sitting on the church steps?

7. Why does Stamp Paid apologize to Paul D?

8. Why had Stamp Paid changed his name from Joshua?

9. Why had Stamp Paid gone to see the young master's wife?

10. What does the red ribbon signify for Stamp Paid?

Answers

1. Schoolteacher had changed life at Sweet Home by taking the guns away from the slaves, not allowing them to offer their thoughts, instituting torture (such as the bit, the iron necklace, and whipping), and killing errant slaves. He revoked whatever small amount of respect Mr. Garner may have given the slaves.

2. The plan for escape from slavery had been that a woman Thirty-Mile Woman knew would wait for the others in the corn when it was high for a day-and-a-half. She would rattle

to signal that the time was right and then take them to the waiting caravan where the others would already be hiding, waiting themselves for this woman who knew the way to freedom.

3. Thirty-Mile Woman had not been caught because Sixo heard schoolteacher, his pupils, and the other four white men and pushed her on her way to safety. She ran into the creek bed while Paul D and Sixo ran the other way. The white men followed them instead of her.

4. Sixo had been burned and shot to death because, even with bound hands, he grabbed one of the rifles and cracked the ribs of one of the white men. Schoolteacher had decided he was not worth saving and had him tied to a tree and burned to death. When Sixo refused to stop laughing while being burned alive, schoolteacher had him shot by one of the white men.

5. When he was captured, Paul D had been tortured by being forced to wear an iron bit in his mouth and an iron three-spoked collar around his neck, even though his hands and feet were shackled.

6. After the white stranger asks Paul D and Stamp Paid how to find Judy, he tells them Paul D should be more respectful than to drink on the steps of a church.

7. Stamp Paid apologized to Paul D because no one in the community offered him a place to stay. He did not know that Reverend Pike had offered, but Paul D refused, just wanting to be alone.

8. Stamp Paid had changed his name from Joshua after the young master had bedded Joshua's wife, Vashti. He felt that by not killing the young master nor his own wife, his dues were paid and he should call himself Stamp Paid since articles were marked "Stamp Paid" when the duty on them was paid.

9. Stamp Paid had gone to see the young master's wife to circumspectly inform her of what her husband was doing. He

could not say it directly since it was the young master's right as slave owner, so he asked the mistress to deliver some trivial message to his wife, describing his wife as wearing a black ribbon around her neck—the one the young master's wife knew her husband had given Vashti, instead of her.

10. For Stamp Paid, the red ribbon signifies the black ribbon young master had given Vashti to wear and, in a larger sense, all the suffering the slaves endured at the hands of their masters.

Suggested Essay Topics

1. Using the text as your reference, explain why you agree or disagree with Sethe that her world is only inside her house and her yard.

2. Explore Denver's innermost thoughts which she reveals in Part Two as explanations for her behavior in Part One. Be certain to validate your opinion with examples from the text.

3. Once again, Sixo is revealed as a slave in body only. Prepare an argument that the spirit cannot be enslaved, using Sixo as your example.

SECTION FOUR

Beloved–Part Three

Pages 239–262

Summary

Denver is excluded from Sethe and Beloved's games after a winter of the three of them playing together. Sethe has been fired for going in to work later and later and, finally, not at all. Denver no longer feels she has to protect Beloved from Sethe, but rather vice-versa. She realizes that if anyone is to provide food for them, since they are becoming lethargic from starvation, it must be she. She forces herself to go out of the yard to Lady Jones who is unable to provide a job, but who—despite Denver's refusal of charity—makes certain her church members share their food with Sethe, Beloved, and Denver.

Since this still does not provide enough food, Denver decides to hire herself out and goes to Cincinnati seeking the Bodwins. Janey Wagon greets her there and arranges a job for her at the Bodwins, sleeping overnight and being available should she be needed. Janey spreads the news of "the sick cousin" visiting the now insane Sethe. Ella soon reasons that this person must be the embodied spirit of Beloved, returned to seek revenge, and organizes the women of the community in a prayer vigil.

During the vigil, the very pregnant Beloved and Sethe come to the door to see who is singing as Denver awaits Mr. Bodwin's arrival on the porch. Sethe, confused, thinks Mr. Bodwin is school-

teacher come to take Beloved again and attacks him with the ice pick she had in her hand.

Analysis

While Sethe spends almost all her time trying to convince Beloved that what she had done was right, Beloved spends her time seeking revenge on Sethe for her murder. Beloved demands and is given; she grows big-bellied with her pregnancy (unseen by Sethe), is given the choicest (and sometimes only) food, and seeks more. She is now the more powerful and lords it over Sethe, whereas before, it was she who hoped for a scrap of Sethe's attention. Denver is no longer useful to her since Beloved now has the power over Sethe she desires, and so is cast aside. Sethe also ignores Denver, having attention and life for no one but Beloved.

As for Denver, she proves herself to be more her father's daughter than her mother's, in that she rises to the occasion when it is needed: to provide the food the women need to keep alive and to prevent her mother from killing Mr. Bodwin. However, she is confused now—is she to keep protecting Beloved from Sethe murdering her again, or is it time to realize that Sethe is pathetic in her insanity and needs to be protected from Beloved?

Study Questions

1. When did Sethe and Beloved begin to exclude Denver?
2. What happened to the $38.00 that was Sethe's life savings?
3. What is Lady Jones' impression of Denver?
4. How do Sethe, Beloved, and Denver survive?
5. How does Denver become reacquainted with the community?
6. Why does Denver go to Cincinnati?
7. What does she tell Janey Wagon of her home life?
8. What is the job Janey obtains for Denver?
9. Why do the women come to 124 Bluestone Road?
10. Why does Sethe attempt to murder Mr. Bodwin?

Answers

1. Sethe and Beloved begin to exclude Denver once Sethe sees the scar on the underside of Beloved's chin. The scar had been caused by the handsaw she used to murder Beloved.

2. The $38.00 which had been Sethe's life savings was squandered on fancy food and garish dress goods they used to make gaudy dresses.

3. Lady Jones recognizes Denver immediately, but her first impression was that Denver was innocent and childlike, rather than a person who acted her chronological age. She was also pleased to see that Denver was not deaf (as Baby Suggs had told her Denver was), since she feels that Denver is quick-minded.

4. When Sethe loses her job and Denver cannot find employment, Sethe, Beloved, and Denver survive by the charity of the committee from Lady Jones' church which makes certain the church members share what they have by leaving food in the yard of those needing it.

5. Denver becomes reacquainted with the community by returning the plates upon which the food was left. The plates have the owners' names on them and Denver visits with the owners as she returns the plates and thanks each of the owners. Each plate owner has another story to tell her about a member of her family, or what it had once been like in her home.

6. Denver goes to Cincinnati to seek the Bodwins. She knows they helped Baby Suggs and then Sethe, and she hopes they will help her find a job.

7. Denver tells Janey Wagon that she has a "sick cousin" staying with her and that her mother is crazy. Denver only tells Janey when she realizes Janey will not allow her to see the Bodwins unless she tells the truth, or something close to it.

8. Janey obtains the job of night caretaker of the Bodwins for Denver, Janey needs to go home to her own family each night, and the Bodwins are getting too old to be by them-

selves throughout the night.

9. The women come to 124 Bluestone Road because Ella organized the 30 of them into a prayer vigil to rid Sethe of the spirit they feel is possessing her and taking her life. Ella was infuriated that the past would come to the present to kill Sethe.

10. Sethe attempts to murder Mr. Bodwin with an ice pick. She had been chipping ice from the block for Beloved and still held it in her hand when she came to see who was singing. She had an insane flashback and thought Mr. Bodwin was schoolteacher coming to take Beloved again.

Suggested Essay Topics

1. Lady Jones immediately recognizes Denver when she calls and wants to help her. While Lady Jones cannot supply a job, her efforts at organizing some relief for the family returns Denver to the community. How does Denver become a viable, welcome member of the community again?

2. Denver was supposedly slow in her thinking, yet it is she who comes to the family's aid when it is necessary. How does Denver demonstrate that she is actually the strongest, not the weakest, member of the family?

3. Sethe and Beloved seem to have changed position in the family. How is it that Sethe is now the beseecher, as Beloved once was, while Beloved is powerful, as Sethe was once? Use the text to validate your opinion.

Pages 263–275

Summary

Paul D returns, reversing the path by which he left: coldhouse to storeroom, storeroom to kitchen, kitchen to bed. Here Boy is home again, a sign that Beloved is surely gone. Stamp Paid says the house is quiet now and Miss Bodwin is going to sell it. Her brother, although against the sale, will not stop her. Mr. Bodwin is still unaware of the attempt on his life, having been mesmerized by the naked black woman on the porch while the scuffle to save him was on.

Paul D asks Denver about her mother. Denver says she's not all right and that Paul D must be careful how he speaks to her. When he gets to the house and finally finds Sethe in the storeroom by following the sound of her humming, it is clear she is laying in bed dying. He recognizes her state from what she had told him about Baby Suggs deciding to die and becomes very angry.

Sethe cries that her best thing—Beloved—is gone. Paul D tells her that SHE, herself, is her best thing and that they need some tomorrows together for they have had too many yesterdays together. Beloved is slowly forgotten, even by those who loved/hated her.

Analysis

Stamp Paid and Paul D have a joint fit of hysterical laughter as they discuss Sethe's attempt on Bodwin's life. This seems appropriate, not for the macabre jokes they make, but because she has ironically attempted to kill the man who kept her alive when she was being tried for Beloved's murder. It is Denver, whose life was saved by Stamp Paid when she was a baby all those years ago, who is one of the first women to wrestle Sethe down (although it was Ella who punched Sethe on the jaw) in order to protect the man who had protected Sethe, now his attempted murderer. It seems that the life cycles have come full circle now. If, indeed, Beloved is the embodied spirit of Sethe's murdered child come back to take revenge on Sethe, what better revenge than to have Sethe kill the man who had saved her life?

Study Questions

1. How did Sethe and Beloved look standing in the doorway?

2. How was Mr. Bodwin saved?

3. Why doesn't he realize there was an attempt on his life?

4. How is Denver faring now?

5. Why does Paul D come back?

6. How does the house look when he enters?

7. Where is Sethe?

8. Why is she preparing to die?

9. What does Paul D tell her at the end of her tears?

10. Why is Beloved forgotten?

Answers

1. Sethe looked unaccountably smaller than Beloved as the two stood in the doorway. While Beloved is visibly pregnant, it is not just her belly, but her whole person, that looks much larger.

2. Mr. Bodwin was saved when Denver, standing on the porch listening to the women sing and waiting for him, wrestles her mother to the ground to take the ice pick from her. Several other women help Denver. Ella punches Sethe on the jaw.

3. Mr. Bodwin was so mesmerized by the sight of the beautiful, naked, pregnant black woman standing on the porch that he was unaware of the attempt on his life. He thought Sethe was going after some of the women who were involved in a fight, when the fight was actually between the women and Sethe to prevent her from killing him.

4. Denver is looking for a job at the shirt factory during the afternoons and still has the night job with the Bodwins. Miss Bodwin is teaching her, and Denver seems to have a young man. She's grown up and is faring well in comparison to what her life had been just a short while ago.

5. Paul D comes back because Sethe is the end of his escapes and his walking. He sees Sethe as the end of his running away and the beginning of his tomorrows.

6. Outside the house, there is a riot of late summer flowers near the coldhouse and on trees, and a short discarded rope is near the washtub, as are many jars of dead lightning bugs.

Inside the house, the railing for the painted white stairs is completely wound with ribbons, bows, and bouquets. Sethe's room is messy, while Denver's is neat.

7. Sethe is in the keeping room, laying in bed, vacant eyed and singing to herself.

8. Sethe is preparing to die because she thinks her best thing is Beloved and Beloved has left her.

9. At the end of her tears, Paul D tells Sethe that she, herself—not Beloved—is her best thing. He also tells her that they have too many yesterdays together and they need more tomorrows together.

10. Beloved is forgotten because she has disappeared. People have already made up their tales about her but no one can validate them with facts. These tales, too, are beginning to be forgotten without someone to verify them.

Suggested Essay Topics

1. Compare and contrast Beloved's power over Sethe in Part Three with Sethe's power over Beloved in Parts One and Two. Use the novel to make a timeline to help you do this.

2. How were each of Paul D's escapes failures? Verify your answer by checking the text.

3. Document the Bodwins' relationship with the three generation of women who lived at 124 Bluestone Road: Baby Suggs, Sethe, and Denver.

Sample Analytical Paper Topics

Topic #1

Mother love is supposedly the strongest and strangest love there is. For example, Sethe maintains throughout the novel that murder was a better alternative than slavery for her children. How may her statement be supported?

Outline

I. Thesis Statement: In *Beloved*, Toni Morrison's protagonist—Sethe—believes death for her children is superior to a life lived in slavery.

II. Treated as Animals in Slavery

    A. Sethe's animal characteristics listed alongside her human ones as an exercise in schoolteacher's classroom

    B. Schoolteacher's nephews suckle Sethe's milk from her breast

    C. Thirty-Mile Woman is almost old enough to "breed"

III. Denied Dominion over Self in Slavery

    A. Baby Suggs' seven babies sold without her consent

    B. Sethe's mother branded

    C. Paul A sold from Sweet Home to meet expenses after Mr. Garner's death

IV.   Torture Used on Slaves

     A.   Sethe whipped when schoolteacher discovered she has told Mrs. Garner that his nephews stole her milk

     B.   Paul D forced to wear the iron bit and three-prong collar after his abortive attempt to escape

     C.   Sixo burned and shot to death after his escape attempt

V.   Usually Denied Family Life in Slavery

     A.   Sethe's mother "given" to many different men

     B.   Baby Suggs permitted to keep only one of her children

     C.   Nan, rather than their mothers, cared for all the slave children

Topic #2

An argument exists that while the body may be enslaved, it is possible to keep the soul free. Sixo effectively demonstrates this argument. What does this statement mean in terms of the novel?

Outline

I.   Thesis Statement: Sixo's spirit was never enslaved.

II.   Refusal to Do Without Love

     A.   20-years-old with no women available at Sweet Home

     B.   Thirty-Mile Woman was just that—thirty miles away

     C.   Sixo found a way to convince her to meet him half way

III.   Refusal to Accept Mental Dominance

     A.   When accused of stealing food, reasoned that he was only "improving the master's property"

     B.   Successfully pilfered blankets for the escape

     C.   Had his own unique theories about the ways of the masters

     D.   Made a convincing argument that Mr. Garner died of being shot in the ear rather than from an exploded ear drum caused by a stroke

IV.   Refusal to Behave like an Animal

    A.   In no way disturbed Sethe when she came to Sweet Home as a girl of 14

    B.   Chose Thirty-Mile Woman for himself and with her agreement

    C.   Rejoiced that Thirty-Mile Woman was pregnant with his child

    D.   Sacrificed himself so that Thirty-Mile Woman could escape the white men hunting them

V.   Refusal to be Limited by Constraints of Slavery

    A.   Would sneak out at night to meet Thirty-Mile Woman

    B.   Devised new and different ways to bake the potatoes he stole

    C.   Laughed as he was being burned as punishment for trying to escape

Topic #3

The spirits of the dead often return to this world for revenge. Beloved has not just come back to be reunited with her mother but to seek revenge for her mother's having murdered her. How do we know this is so?

Outline

I.   Thesis Statement: Beloved seeks revenge for her murder.

II.   Beloved is the Older, Murdered Daughter's Re-embodiment

    A.   Hums the song Sethe had made up for her children

    B.   Asks where Sethe's diamonds (crystal earrings) are

    C.   Has lines on her forehead from where Sethe held her head back in order to slit her throat

III.   Beloved Seduces Her Mother's Lover

    A.   "Shines" on Paul D without either Sethe or Denver seeing

    B.   Actively resents the time and energy Sethe spends on

Paul D

  C. Magically forces Paul D to move out of the house

  D. Taunts him into having sex with her repeatedly

IV. Beloved is Cruel to her Mother

  A. Attempts to spiritually choke her in The Clearing where Baby Suggs had led the congregation

  B. Argues with Sethe that she did not have to be murdered in order to be saved

  C. Willfully demands the best and choicest food, even when the three women were starving

  D. Toward the end of her pregnancy and residence at 124 Bluestone Road, makes Sethe her slave

V. Sethe's Relationship with Denver is Changed

  A. Beloved resents Denver's place in her mother's attentions

  B. Drives Sethe insane, causing Denver to leave the home to support them

  C. Demands all of Denver's attention until she has all of Sethe's, then disregards Denver—effectively leaving Denver without any attention

Topic #4

Sometimes circumstances bring out the best in us and force maturity where there had been none before. Such is the case with Denver, who seems to have had no alternative but to grow up when Sethe becomes insane and Beloved a burden. How may this be proven from the book?

Outline

I. Thesis Statement: Denver is forced to mature by the circumstances surrounding her.

II. Denver's Behavior Prior to Beloved's Appearance

  A. Lady Jones accepted that she was deaf, as Baby Suggs maintained, when Denver disappeared from school

     B.   Sethe apologizes to Paul D for her behavior

     C.   Is easily won over by Paul D with a trip to the carnival

     D.   Docilely follows her mother's instructions on a daily basis

III. Changes in Behavior Upon Beloved's Appearance

     A.   Takes total charge of Beloved's recuperation

     B.   Once Beloved is well, takes it upon herself to keep Beloved entertained and supplied with sweets

     C.   Shares her secret place with Beloved

     D.   Seems to forget about arguing with Paul D except when he suggests that Beloved should be leaving

IV. Assumption of Responsibility

     A.   At first, protects only herself from Sethe and the fear that Sethe may murder her, as she had Beloved

     B.   Once Beloved appears, protects her from Sethe as well

     C.   After Beloved has power over Sethe, protects Sethe from Beloved

     D.   Prevents Sethe from murdering Mr. Bodwin

V. The Final Product

     A.   Left the home to work at the Bodwins nightly

     B.   Accepts that Paul D will be seeing her mother

     C.   Is looking for an afternoon job

     D.   Has a young man she cares for

     E.   Has re-integrated herself with the community

Topic #5

Older people have different ways of dealing with their impending deaths; Stamp Paid and Baby Suggs had differing reactions to the weariness that made them flirt with death. How did they differ?

Outline

I. Thesis Statement: Baby Suggs and Stamp Paid had different reactions to the weariness that tells us death may be approaching.

II. Baby Suggs' Reactions

   A. Stopped leading her congregation in The Clearing

   B. Slowly stopped leaving her yard

   C. For a number of years, refused to leave her bed in the house

   D. Spent her remaining years concentrating on colors

III. Stamp Paid's Reactions

   A. Realized his bone-marrow weariness must have been what Baby Suggs had felt

   B. Dismayed that he had gotten angry with Baby Suggs over her withdrawal from the world

   C. Understands how the distant past holds such vivid memories for him

IV. Effects of Baby Suggs' Withdrawal

   A. Friendship with Stamp Paid lapses

   B. Congregation is no longer

   C. Since the inhabitants of 124 Bluestone Road are still being shunned, all three women lose contact with the community

V. Effects of Stamp Paid's Bone-Marrow Weariness

   A. Goes to tell Sethe that he read Paul D the newspaper article

   B. Looks for Paul D in an effort to find out who Beloved is

   C. Remembers his part in saving Denver's life

   D. Is proud of his part in the Underground Railroad

SECTION SIX

Bibliography

Bloom, Harold, ed. *Modern Critical Views: Toni Morrison*. New York: Chelsea House Publishers, 1990.

Dubois, W.E.B. *Black Reconstruction in America: 1860–1880*. New York: Atheneum, 1992.

Gates, Henry Louis Jr. and Appiah, K.A., ed. *Toni Morrison: Critical Perspectives Past and Present*. New York: Amistad Press, Inc., 1993.

Lingley, Charles Ramsdell and Foley, Allen Richard. *Since the Civil War–Third Edition*. New York: Century Co., Inc., 1935.

McKay, Nellie Y., ed. *Critical Essays on Toni Morrison*. Massachusetts: G.K. Hall & Co., 1988.

Stampp, Kenneth M. *The Era of Reconstruction 1865–1877*. New York: Alfred Knopf, 1966.

Videos:

Profile of a Writer: Toni Morrison, Alan Benson, R.M. Arts, 52 min., Public Media, Inc., 1987.

A Conversation with Toni Morrison, Matteo Bellinelli, 25 min., RTSI–Swiss Television, "In Black and White: Part 3."

REA's **Test Preps**
The Best in Test Preparation

REA "Test Preps" are far **more** comprehensive than any other test preparation series
Each book contains up to **eight** full-length practice exams based on the most recent exams
Every type of question likely to be given on the exams is included
Answers are accompanied by **full** and **detailed** explanations

REA has published over 60 Test Preparation volumes in several series. They include:

Advanced Placement Exams (APs)
Biology
Calculus AB & Calculus BC
Chemistry
Computer Science
English Language & Composition
English Literature & Composition
European History
Government & Politics
Physics
Psychology
Spanish Language
United States History

College Level Examination Program (CLEP)
American History I
Analysis & Interpretation of Literature
College Algebra
Freshman College Composition
General Examinations
Human Growth and Development
Introductory Sociology
Principles of Marketing

SAT II: Subject Tests
American History
Biology
Chemistry
French
German
Literature

SAT II: Subject Tests (continued)
Mathematics Level IC, IIC
Physics
Spanish
Writing

Graduate Record Exams (GREs)
Biology
Chemistry
Computer Science
Economics
Engineering
General
History
Literature in English
Mathematics
Physics
Political Science
Psychology
Sociology

ACT - American College Testing Assessment

ASVAB - Armed Service Vocational Aptitude Battery

CBEST - California Basic Educational Skills Test

CDL - Commercial Driver's License Exam

CLAST - College Level Academic Skills Test

ELM - Entry Level Mathematics

ExCET - Exam for Certification of Educators in Texas

FE (EIT) - Fundamentals of Engineering Exam

FE Review - Fundamentals of Engineering Review

GED - High School Equivalency Diploma Exam (US & Canadian editions)

GMAT - Graduate Management Admission Test

LSAT - Law School Admission Test

MAT - Miller Analogies Test

MCAT - Medical College Admission Test

MSAT - Multiple Subjects Assessment for Teachers

NTE - National Teachers Exam

PPST - Pre-Professional Skills Tests

PSAT - Preliminary Scholastic Assessment Test

SAT I - Reasoning Test

SAT I - Quick Study & Review

TASP - Texas Academic Skills Program

TOEFL - Test of English as a Foreign Language

RESEARCH & EDUCATION ASSOCIATION
61 Ethel Road W. • Piscataway, New Jersey 08854
Phone: (908) 819-8880

Please send me more information about your Test Prep Books

Name _____

Address _____

City _____ State _____ Zip _____

Available at your local bookstore or order directly from us by sending in coupon below.

THE BEST TEST PREPARATION FOR THE

AP
ADVANCED
PLACEMENT
EXAMINATION

ENGLISH
Literature & Composition

by Pauline Beard, Ph.D. • Robert Liftig, Ed.D. • James Malek, Ph.D. •
James Maloney, M.A. • Joanne Miller, M.A. • Peter Trenouth, M.A. • Mattie Williams, M.A.

6 Full-Length Exams
➤ Every question based on the current exams
➤ The ONLY test preparation book with detailed explanations to every question
➤ Far more comprehensive than any other test preparation book

Includes a COMPREHENSIVE AP COURSE REVIEW,
emphasizing all areas of literature & composition found on the exam

REA *Research & Education Association*

Available at your local bookstore or order directly from us by sending in coupon below.

MAXnotes

REA's Literature Study Guide.

MAXnotes™ are student-friendly. They offer a fresh look at masterpieces of literature, presented in a lively and interesting fashion. **MAXnotes**™ offer the essentials of what you should know about the work, including outlines, explanations and discussions of the plot, character lists, analyses, and historical context. **MAXnotes**™ are designed to help you think independently about literary works by raising various issues and thought-provoking ideas and questions. Written by literary experts who currently teach the subject, **MAXnotes**™ enhance your understanding and enjoyment of the work.

Available **MAXnotes**™ include the following:

Absalom, Absalom!	Heart of Darkness	Of Mice and Men
The Aeneid of Virgil	Henry IV, Part I	On the Road
Animal Farm	Henry V	Othello
Antony and Cleopatra	The House on Mango Street	Paradise Lost
As I Lay Dying	Huckleberry Finn	A Passage to India
As You Like It	I Know Why the Caged	Plato's Republic
The Autobiography of	Bird Sings	Portrait of a Lady
Malcolm X	The Iliad	A Portrait of the Artist
The Awakening	Invisible Man	as a Young Man
Beloved	Jane Eyre	Pride and Prejudice
Beowulf	Jazz	A Raisin in the Sun
Billy Budd	The Joy Luck Club	Richard II
The Bluest Eye, A Novel	Jude the Obscure	Romeo and Juliet
Brave New World	Julius Caesar	The Scarlet Letter
The Canterbury Tales	King Lear	Sir Gawain and the
The Catcher in the Rye	Les Misérables	Green Knight
The Color Purple	Lord of the Flies	Slaughterhouse-Five
The Crucible	Macbeth	Song of Solomon
Death in Venice	The Merchant of Venice	The Sound and the Fury
Death of a Salesman	The Metamorphoses of Ovid	The Stranger
The Divine Comedy I: Inferno	The Metamorphosis	The Sun Also Rises
Dubliners	Middlemarch	A Tale of Two Cities
Emma	A Midsummer Night's Dream	Taming of the Shrew
Euripedes' Electra & Medea	Moby-Dick	The Tempest
Frankenstein	Moll Flanders	Tess of the D'Urbervilles
Gone with the Wind	Mrs. Dalloway	Their Eyes Were Watching God
The Grapes of Wrath	Much Ado About Nothing	To Kill a Mockingbird
Great Expectations	My Antonia	To the Lighthouse
The Great Gatsby	Native Son	Twelfth Night
Gulliver's Travels	1984	Uncle Tom's Cabin
Hamlet	The Odyssey	Waiting for Godot
Hard Times	Oedipus Trilogy	Wuthering Heights

RESEARCH & EDUCATION ASSOCIATION
61 Ethel Road W. • Piscataway, New Jersey 08854
Phone: (908) 819-8880

Please send me more information about MAXnotes™.

Name _____

Address _____

City _____ State _____ Zip_____